W9-BNQ-410

# James McNair's
# PIE
## COOKBOOK

Photography by Patricia Brabant

Chronicle Books · San Francisco

Copyright © 1989 by James McNair.
All rights reserved. No portion of this book may
be reproduced by any means without permission
in writing from the publisher.

Printed in Japan

Library of Congress
Cataloging-in-Publication Data
McNair, James K.
[Pie cookbook]
James McNair's Pie Cookbook
/ James McNair;
/ photography by Patricia Brabant.
p. cm.
Includes index.
ISBN 0-87701-600-3
ISBN 0-87701-595-3 (pbk.)
1. Pies  I. Title.
II. Title: Pie cookbook.
TX773.M35 1989
641.8'652—dc20
89-34354 CIP


Distributed in Canada by
Raincoast Books
112 East Third Avenue
Vancouver, British Columbia V5T 1C8

10 9 8 7 6 5 4 3 2 1

Chronicle Books
275 Fifth Street
San Francisco, California 94103

For Gregg King, one of my longest-running intimate friends, who adores
Cherry Cream Pie. His success as a New York designer and as a sensitive,
caring man makes me pleased that I cooked all those pies for him while he
was growing up a few years behind me in Jonesville, Louisiana.

**Produced by The Rockpile Press, San Francisco and Lake Tahoe**

**Art direction, photographic and food styling, and book design by
James McNair**

**Editorial production assistance by Lin Cotton**

**Studio kitchen assistance by Ellen Quan**

**Photography assistance by Carrie Loyd and M. J. Murphy**

**Typography and mechanical production by Cleve Gallat and
Don Kruse of CTA Graphics**

# CONTENTS

# INTRODUCTION

Like no other dessert, except possibly puddings, pie means *home* to most of us.

How fondly I recall my mother's chocolate pie, warm from the oven, as well as her lemon meringue, which we also ate still warm. Years and miles from home, I've always been disappointed with cold chocolate pie and the thick gluelike lemon pie in most restaurants.

Over the years I've relived moments in my Grandmother Keith's kitchen whenever I've made her cherry cream pie, and I've turned my Grandmother McNair's fantastic banana pudding into a delectable pie.

When I was growing up in pecan pie country, every good cook I knew in Louisiana's Catahoula Parish had his or her own way of making this rich concoction. But my fifth-grade school teacher, Eula Cain, made my favorite version, which she always brought to church dinners-on-the-ground. Decades after she gave me her recipe, I found it verbatim in an old cookbook, but it remains Miss Eula's pie to me.

During my senior year in college, I shared an apartment with Ragan Courtney and Jerry Myrick. Once one of us remarked that we'd never had enough lemon icebox pie, that rich concoction made with condensed milk, eggs, and lemon juice. We all regretted that every time it was brought to church potlucks or served at home it had to be cut into too many pieces. That afternoon I remedied the situation, and after dinner I placed a whole pie and a fork in front of each of us. What a sweet memory!

Just as the French are masters of the tart, American cooks are the undisputed queens and kings of pie baking. This book is joyfully devoted to America's favorite dessert, the one we do better than anyone else.

## WHAT IS A PIE, ANYWAY?

Webster says the name for America's favorite dessert probably came from the magpie bird, which was commonly called "pie." Just as the bird brought bits of everything home to his nest, so pies originated as simple sweets made with whatever was on hand or in seasonal abundance.

A *sweet pie* is defined as a dessert with either an under crust, an upper crust, or both. Through the years we have developed a wide variety of fillings, types of crusts, and methods of putting them together. This book includes my favorite traditional pies, some nostalgic recipes from my childhood, and a few newfangled ideas that could become part of America's pie repertoire.

# MAKING PERFECT PIES

We've all heard certain activities referred to as being "as easy as pie," yet many people don't see making a pie as an easy process. I know a number of excellent cooks who balk at making pies, or more exactly, pie crusts. Instead of mastering the simple skills required for perfect flaky pastry, they reach for a frozen crust or buy ready-made pies.

The next several pages are designed to alleviate any fears and remove any mystery associated with pie baking, as well as to offer some new ideas for the accomplished pie maker. Whether you're a novice or a seasoned cook, the step-by-step directions will show you how to turn out perfect pies that are far more delicious than any pie you can purchase. Once you've learned to make a perfect crust, which takes only minutes to prepare, you can enjoy a whole new world of cooking pleasure.

## INGREDIENTS

**FLOUR.** All-purpose flour, a blend of hard and soft wheats, is fine for pie crusts. Unbleached all-purpose flour has better flavor and more nutritional value than its bleached counterpart. It is not necessary to sift today's flour when making pastry.

**FAT.** Flaky crusts can be made from a variety of fats. I prefer all butter for its special flavor, even though the crust is not quite as flaky as those made from solid vegetable shortening, including margarine. The flakiest pastry is made with lard; however, both butter and lard should be avoided by anyone with a cholesterol problem. Butter and other fats can be mixed together to assure a tender, flaky crust that contains some of the rich taste of butter. All fats should be very well chilled before using in pastry.

Polyunsaturated vegetable oil produces a satisfactory crust that is good for those on low-cholesterol diets. For additional information, see the sidebar on choosing a fat on page 11.

# EQUIPMENT

You can probably make pies with the equipment already in your kitchen, but here are a few items that greatly aid the process, listed in the usual order in which they are used in baking.

**FOOD PROCESSOR.** Makes blending pastry quick and easy as long as you're careful not to overwork the dough. Makes producing crumbs for crumb crusts or finely chopped nuts for a nut crust a snap.

**PASTRY BLENDER.** This simple device, with curved wire blades attached to a wooden handle, cuts fat into dry ingredients, although fingertips do the job faster with less chance of overworking the pastry.

**WAXED PAPER.** Rolling dough between two sheets of waxed paper makes kitchen cleanup much easier. Boxed pre-cut, pull-out sheets from commercial kitchen suppliers are more convenient than rolls.

**ROLLING SURFACE.** Smooth wooden or plastic laminate countertops work well, provided you haven't used them for cutting onions or other strongly flavored foods. A pastry board fashioned of marble, rigid plastic, or wood is convenient. Rolling between waxed paper sheets eliminates the need for flouring surfaces or for pastry cloths.

**ROLLING PIN.** Choose a straight smooth pin of wood or marble; handles are optional. Cloth rolling-pin sleeves seem unnecessary when a dusting of flour accomplishes the same purpose. Rolling pastry between two sheets of waxed paper makes cleaning the pin easy; pins should be wiped clean, never washed.

**DOUGH SCRAPER.** A flexible metal blade with a wooden handle, useful for cleaning up dough residue from work surfaces.

**PIE PANS.** Stock several 8- or 9-inch pans and a couple of 10-inch pans for serving larger groups. Heat-resistant glass pans allow for a peek at how the bottom crust is cooking. Since glass pans distribute heat faster than their metal counterparts, they prevent filled bottom crusts from becoming soggy during baking. Heavy-duty aluminum pans darkened from use also produce excellent results. Shiny new pans reflect heat, thereby producing undercooked bottom crusts; they should be washed and dried, then rubbed with vegetable oil and baked empty at 425° for about 30 minutes. On the other hand, black pans may brown crusts too rapidly. Thin metal pans cook the outside of the crust too fast, preventing proper interior cooking, although throw-away foil pans can be used successfully with crumb crusts and completely pre-baked crusts. Nonstick pans are not recommended because you cannot cut and serve pies without scratching and harming the coating.

**ALUMINUM FOIL OR BAKING PARCHMENT.** Keep on hand for lining pie shells for pre-baking.

**PIE WEIGHTS.** Metal, ceramic, or clay pie weights, available in cookware stores, can be used to fill a pie shell for pre-baking; dried beans work just as well.

**PASTRY CUTTERS.** Rolling cutting wheels come with either straight edges or fluted edges to make cutting pastry strips for lattice or other decorative designs a breeze. Small pizza cutters will do the same thing.

**RULER.** A standard 12-inch ruler is very helpful in measuring diameters or to use as a guide for straight pastry strips.

**COOKIE CUTTERS.** An assortment of shapes allows for whimsical top crusts. Tiny hors d'oeuvres cutters are useful for cutting fanciful shapes for pie rim decorations.

**PASTRY BRUSHES.** Choose brushes with soft bristles for glazing crusts.

**ELECTRIC MIXER.** A hand-held mixer does a fine job of beating meringue or fillings.

**PIE SERVER.** For easy serving, choose a spatula with a triangular blade.

**SALT. A pinch of salt is added to pie pastry not only for flavor but for a richer color in the baked crust.**

**LIQUID. Most pie crusts call for water to moisten the flour-fat mixture. Water, beaten egg, or any other additions to the crust must be ice cold to prevent the fat from starting to melt. Use liquid sparingly, adding it a bit at a time; too much creates tough pastry.**

**FILLINGS. As with all good cooking, use only the freshest and finest ingredients available. You don't want to create a perfect crust and skimp on the fillings.**

# Basic Pie Crust

3 cups all-purpose flour,
    preferably unbleached
1 teaspoon salt
2 teaspoons granulated sugar
1 cup (2 sticks) cold unsalted butter
    or other fat (page 11), alone or
    in combination, cut into small
    pieces (if mixing in a food
    processor the fat should
    be frozen)
½ cup or more ice water

This recipe yields enough flaky pastry for two single-crust pies or a double-crust pie with enough left over for cutout garnishes. If you're making only one pie without a top crust, either cut the recipe in half or go ahead and roll out two crusts. Place the extra one either flat or pressed into a pie pan in a large self-sealing bag and freeze for up to several weeks.

When I want to make fanciful decorations that require more handling of the dough than a simple bottom crust, I make the Sweet Crust variation; the egg yolks make it easy to work with and give the sturdy pastry a rich golden color.

To mix the pastry by hand, combine the flour, salt, and sugar in a bowl and mix well. Using a pastry blender, 2 dinner knives, or your fingertips, cut the butter or other fat into the dry ingredients as quickly as possible until the mixture resembles coarse bread crumbs. Sprinkle ½ cup of the ice water over the mixture and combine with a fork or your fingertips just until the dough holds together. If the dough seems too crumbly, add more ice water, 1 tablespoon at a time.

To mix the pastry in a food processor, combine the flour, salt, and sugar in the work bowl. Using the steel blade, process for 1 or 2 seconds to mix the dry ingredients. Add the butter or other fat and cut into the dry ingredients by turning the processor on and off with quick pulses just until the mixture resembles coarse bread crumbs. Sprinkle ½ cup of the ice water over the mixture and turn the motor on and off with quick pulses just until the mixture begins to mass together. The dough should be crumbly but not dry. If the mixture seems too crumbly, add more ice water, 1 tablespoon at a time.

Whether mixed by hand or in a food processor, turn half of the mixture onto a sheet of waxed paper, gather into a ball, and press into a thick flat disk about 5 inches in diameter. Bring the paper around to enclose the dough and refrigerate for about 15 minutes to "relax" the dough for a more tender crust.

Follow directions on the next several pages for rolling and finishing crusts.

**Makes pastry for one 8- to 10-inch double-crust pie, or two 8- to 10-inch single pie shells.**

# FLAVORFUL VARIATIONS

**ALMOND OR VANILLA CRUST.** For a delicately almond-flavored crust to use with egg custard or nut pies, add ½ teaspoon almond extract along with the ice water. For flavorful crust that goes well with berry or other fruit pies, add 1 teaspoon vanilla extract along with the ice water, or substitute vanilla-sugar for the regular sugar.

**BROWN SUGAR CRUST.** Substitute brown sugar for the granulated and add ½ teaspoon ground cinnamon along with the salt.

**CHEDDAR CRUST.** For an occasional change of pace with apple or pear pie, reduce the butter to ½ cup and stir in 1 cup grated Cheddar cheese after cutting in the butter.

**CHOCOLATE CRUST.** Whenever a chocolate crust seems compatible with the filling, add ¼ cup powdered cocoa to the flour.

**CORNMEAL CRUST.** For a bright yellow crust with a bit of crunch and flavor that goes well with pumpkin, nut, or other autumn pies, substitute 1 cup finely ground yellow cornmeal for 1 cup of the flour; a bit more ice water may be required.

**CREAM CHEESE CRUST.** Cream cheese or sour cream can be used in place of half of the butter or other fat for a delicate texture and slightly tart flavor.

**SPICE CRUST.** For a spicy crust that goes well with fruit pies, add about ½ teaspoon freshly grated nutmeg or ground cinnamon, cloves, or ginger to the flour and salt mixture.

**SWEET CRUST.** For a sweeter pre-baked shell to fill with a stirred custard, cream, or mousse filling, decrease the salt to ½ teaspoon, increase the sugar to 3 tablespoons, and beat 2 cold egg yolks with the ice water.

**WHOLE-WHEAT CRUST.** For a crunchy crust that is compatible with heavy fillings such as pumpkin or mincemeat, substitute all or half whole-wheat pastry flour for the regular flour and add 1 teaspoon baking powder along with the salt.

## CHOOSING A FAT

**BUTTER.** Crusts made with all butter are the most flavorful and the easiest to blend and handle. Although butter crusts are not quite as tender or flaky as a crust made with vegetable shortening, margarine, or lard, the special flavor makes them my standard choice. Butter can be combined in equal portions with shortening or lard for crusts that will provide some of the flavor of butter and some of the flakiness that the other fats offer.

**LARD.** Rendered lard assures the tenderest and flakiest crust with a flavor that is especially compatible with apples, dried fruits, or mincemeat. Use in place of all or part of the butter in the basic recipe.

**SOLID SHORTENING.** All-vegetable shortening or margarine has as many calories as butter, but is low in cholesterol and produces a very flaky, fragile crust. The resulting bland taste is often preferred when filling a pie with ultra-rich concoctions. Use in place of all or part of the butter in the basic recipe.

**OIL.** Polyunsaturated vegetable oil produces a non-cholesterol crust, but lacks the luxurious flavor of butter crusts and the flakiness of those made with solid shortening. Use ⅔ cup oil instead of ¾ cup butter in the basic recipe.

# Forming Pie Crusts

## TIPS FOR PERFECT PASTRY

**All fat and liquid ingredients must be very cold; if using a food processor for mixing, freeze the fats before using.**

**When mixing butter and solid shortening or any two types of fat together in a crust, it is best to soften the fats, blend them, and chill before using.**

**Mix the ingredients as quickly as possible. Flaky pastry results from pockets of shortening left to melt in between flour paste layers; over-mixing results in a tough crust.**

**Chill the pastry before rolling out and again before baking.**

**When touching dough, be sure your hands are cold; an occasional rinse in cold water keeps them the right temperature.**

**When rolling out and assembling crusts, handle the pastry as quickly and as little as possible. If the butter or other fat gets too soft, it will be absorbed by the flour, resulting in a crust that is heavy and tough.**

To roll out the dough, remove one piece of the chilled pastry (prepared from the preceding recipe) from the refrigerator and place it in the middle of a piece of waxed paper about 12 inches square. Cover the pastry with a second waxed paper sheet. Allow to soften for about 5 minutes. Roll dough from the center toward the edges, reducing the pressure as you near the edges, to form a circle about 1/8 inch thick. Use an empty pie pan as a guide; the piece of dough should be 1 or 2 inches larger than the top of the pan. Replace waxed paper when it wrinkles.

Alternatively, place the chilled dough on a lightly floured surface. Sprinkle the top with a little flour and dust the rolling pin with flour. Roll as above, lifting dough and giving it a quarter turn after each roll. Add a bit more flour as necessary.

If dough breaks during rolling, brush the tear with a bit of cold water and cover with a piece of rolled dough cut from the edge of the circle. Avoid rerolling, as it toughens dough.

To line a pie pan, discard the top layer of waxed paper. Invert the dough into the pan and peel away the waxed paper. Beginning at the center of the pan and working toward the edges and up the sides, press the dough lightly into the pan with your fingertips.

**Rolling.**

**Trimming.**

**Folding.**

To finish off a single-crust pie shell or the bottom crust of a double-crust pie shell, cut the edge of the pastry with a small sharp knife or kitchen scissors so it hangs evenly about 1 inch past the outer edge of the pan. Although countless pie recipes direct you to fold the edges of the dough under itself so it is even with the outside edge of the pan, I find that folding the dough down over itself toward the inside of the pan is easier. Smooth the perimeter with your fingertips to form a thick raised rim. Form attractive edges such as those suggested on the next two pages. Chill in the refrigerator or freezer for about 30 minutes before baking or filling. At this point, crusts in pans also can be placed in heavy-duty, self-sealing plastic bags and frozen for up to several weeks.

**Appliqué.**

**Braid.**

**Checkerboard.**

**Feather.**

# Decorating Edges

In addition to the standard practice of pressing the tines of a fork into smoothed pastry all the way around the perimeter to create a fluted edging, use these suggestions to get your own creativity flowing.

**APPLIQUÉ.** Cut out the rolled top sheet of pastry with tiny aspic cutters. Brush the rim of the crust with cold water and apply the cutouts, slightly overlapping. Gently press to stick the cutouts to the rim.

**BRAID.** Cut long strips of extra dough about ¼ inch wide. Braid 2 or 3 strips together to interlock and apply to the moistened rim.

**CHECKERBOARD.** Use a sharp knife to cut across the rim at ½-inch intervals. Alternately fold every other piece in towards the center.

**FEATHER.** Use a sharp pair of kitchen scissors to snip slanted incisions every ¼ inch around the perimeter of the pastry.

Flute.

Point.

Scallop.

Spoon Scallop.

**FLUTE.** Position an index finger on the outside of the pastry rim, pointing diagonally inward. Use the index finger and thumb of the other hand to push the pastry against the finger to form wide flutes.

**POINT.** Position an index finger on the inside of the pastry rim, pointing out. With the index finger and thumb of the other hand, crimp the pastry into pronounced points that go outward.

**SCALLOP.** Place the index finger of one hand on the edge of the rim, pointing in. Use the index finger and the thumb of the other hand to move the dough inward to form scallops around the perimeter.

**SPOON SCALLOP.** Press the rounded tip of a spoon into the rim to form a scallop pattern. If desired, move the spoon down and repeat with a smaller scallop.

**Weighting.**

# Pre-baking, Filling, and Topping

After forming and chilling the pie crust pastry as directed on the preceding pages, completely pre-bake, or "blind-bake," a pie shell that is to be filled with a stirred custard, cream, mousse, or other ready-to-eat fillings.

To assure very crisp crusts on pies that will be filled and then baked, I strongly recommend pre-baking. In this departure from standard pie-cooking techniques, the heat penetrates the partially cooked shell during further baking and cooks the filling without overcooking the bottom crust; the crust rim can be covered with aluminum foil to prevent excess browning. If you don't wish to go to this extra bit of trouble, brushing the inside of the chilled uncooked crust with lightly beaten egg white helps seal the pastry, making it difficult for the filling to penetrate and soften.

To completely or partially pre-bake a pie shell, preheat an oven to 400° F.

Cut a sheet of baking parchment or aluminum foil about 2 inches larger than the diameter of the pie. Press it into the pastry shell and fill it with pie weights, dried beans, or rice. Bake until the rim of the crust feels just set to the touch, about 7 to 10 minutes. Remove from the oven and carefully lift the parchment or foil and the weights from the crust.

Prick the bottom and sides of the pie crust in several places with the tines of a fork. Return the shell to the oven. Check the crust several times during baking and prick it again with a fork if the crust puffs up. For a shell that will be filled and baked further, cook until the crust is almost done but not completely browned, about 5 to 10 minutes longer. For a shell that will be filled with a ready-to-eat filling, cook until golden brown, about 15 minutes more after returning to the oven. Position strips of aluminum foil around the edge of crusts, if it begins to get too brown.

**Cooling.** **Filling.** **Topping.**

Remove the crust from the oven and cool completely before filling; cooling prevents soggy crusts.

Single-crust pies may be filled after both the shell and the filling are cooled for about 15 minutes or as directed in recipes. For the crispest crust, fill as close to the time the pie will be eaten as possible.

For meringue-topped filled pies, use the recipe on page 92.

**Covering.**

**Decorating.**

To fill and top a completely covered double-crust pie, roll out the second piece of dough into a rough circle a little thinner than the bottom crust. Use an empty pie pan to cut the dough into a circle slightly larger all around than the top of the pie. Fill the partially pre-baked pie shell as directed in the recipe. If splits occur in the crust during baking, mend by covering with a thin layer of almond paste, a technique first suggested some years ago by the great American baker, Maida Heatter. Brush the rim of the filled pie with lightly beaten egg white. (If you prefer to start with a raw crust, brush the rim of the filled pie with water.) Cover the pie with the top crust and trim it even with the bottom crust. Press the edges together to seal.

With a sharp knife, cut slits or designs into the top to serve as air vents. If desired, cut out decorations such as leaves, flowers, stars, or other fanciful or geometric shapes with a knife or cookie cutters. Brush the bottom of each with a little cold water and stick onto the top crust in an attractive pattern.

**Cutouts.**  **Lattice.**  **Glazing.**

To partially cover a pie, which is especially appropriate when the filling is colorful or particularly attractive, as with a berry pie, roll out the second piece of dough and fill the pre-baked shell as directed in recipe. For a lattice, striped, or spiral design, use a plain or fluted rolling pastry cutter or sharp knife with a ruler as a guide to cut the dough sheet into long thin strips. Arrange on the top of the pie in a desired pattern. Trim the edges of the strips to meet the rim of the pie. Lift the strips and brush the underside with water or beaten egg white and press onto the rim of the bottom crust.

The pie may also be covered with free-form or cookie-cutter cutouts. Arrange them slightly overlapping to cover most of the pie, leaving spaces for air vents in between, or scatter them over the top in any design you wish.

For a richer baked color, brush the exposed crust with cream, milk, or lightly beaten egg; beaten egg yolk mixed with a bit of water or cream produces a deep golden finish. For a crackle glaze, sprinkle with granulated sugar or a flavored sugar such as vanilla-sugar.

# Seasonal Pies

The following pies represent the best of each season's bounty. First comes tart spring rhubarb, followed by sweet summer berries and juicy peaches. Autumn pies are made from crisp apples, tangy cranberries, and an abundant harvest of nuts. Zesty citrus and luscious tropical imports brighten the winter cooking scene.

Even though some of these ingredients are now available all year long, they are at their peak of flavor during their natural season.

# Rhubarb Mousse Pie

Some years ago I enjoyed a lovely visit with Sir Cecil Beaton at his English country house. A mousse made of fresh rhubarb from his extensive garden was the highlight of lunch, and became the inspiration for this pie.

Prepare the crust as directed on page 90 or 91 and set aside to cool.

Combine the rhubarb and water in a saucepan over medium heat. Bring to a boil, cover, and cook, stirring occasionally, until the rhubarb is very tender, about 5 minutes. Strain and reserve liquid.

Transfer the rhubarb to a food processor or blender, add ½ cup of the sugar, the lemon juice, and gelatin and purée until smooth. Bring the reserved liquid to a boil and add ⅓ cup of it to the rhubarb mixture and process to blend. Set aside to cool.

Combine the egg yolks and the remaining ¾ cup of the sugar in the top container of a double boiler set over simmering water. Cook, stirring or whisking constantly, until the mixture is smooth and thick and just hot to the touch. Set in a bowl of ice and whisk the mixture until cool. Stir in the rhubarb mixture and let stand, stirring frequently, until the mixture reaches the consistency of lightly whipped cream.

Whip the cream until quite thick but not stiff. Fold it into the rhubarb mixture and pour into the cooled pie shell. Smooth the top, cover loosely, and refrigerate until firm enough to slice, about 2 to 3 hours.

Just before serving, garnish with whipped cream and violets, if desired.

**Makes one 9-inch pie; serves 6 to 8.**

Cookie Crumb Crust (page 90),
    or Meringue Crust (page 91)
6 cups chopped tender young
    rhubarb
½ cup water
1¼ cups granulated sugar
2 tablespoons freshly squeezed
    lemon juice
1 scant tablespoon (1 envelope)
    unflavored gelatin
3 egg yolks
1 cup heavy (whipping) cream
Whipped cream for garnish (optional)
Pesticide-free sweet violets
    for garnish (optional)

# Glazed Strawberry-Raspberry Pie

½ recipe Basic Pie Crust (page 10),
   preferably Sweet Crust variation
   (page 11)
3 cups strawberries, hulled
2 cups raspberries
1 tablespoon freshly squeezed
   lemon juice
1 cup granulated sugar
3 tablespoons cornstarch

While most berries bake into a delicious filling for a double-crust pie, strawberries are at their best when uncooked berries are tossed with a thickened mixture of mashed berries, then poured into a completely baked crisp shell. All strawberries or just raspberries make a delicious pie, but the combination is even better. Use this same technique to make glazed-fruit pies from mango, papaya, peaches, or other soft fruits.

**This pie calls for plenty of softly whipped cream.**

As directed beginning on page 10, prepare the pastry, roll out, line a 9-inch pie pan, and bake completely. Cool the pie shell about 15 minutes before filling.

Place 2½ cups of the berries in a large heavy pan and mash with the back of a wooden spoon or a fork. Sprinkle with the lemon juice and stir in the sugar and cornstarch. Place over medium-low heat and cook, stirring constantly, until the mixture comes to a boil and thickens, about 8 minutes. Remove from the heat to cool to lukewarm.

Slice the remaining strawberries, if large, and fold them and the remaining raspberries into the cooled berry mixture. Spoon into the cooled pie shell. Serve at room temperature.

**Makes one 9-inch pie; serves 6 to 8.**

# Lemony Berry Pie

Basic Pie Crust (page 10)
5 cups stemmed blueberries
1 cup granulated sugar
6 tablespoons all-purpose flour,
  preferably unbleached
½ teaspoon freshly grated nutmeg
¼ teaspoon ground cinnamon
2 tablespoons grated or minced
  lemon zest
2 tablespoons freshly squeezed
  lemon juice
2 tablespoons unsalted butter,
  cut into small pieces
1 egg white, lightly beaten
1 egg lightly beaten with 2 tablespoons
  heavy (whipping) cream for
  glazing
Granulated sugar for sprinkling

This recipe using blueberries adapts to huckleberries, gooseberries, raspberries, blackberries, or other berries as well as grapes and pitted sweet or sour cherries. Vary the amount of sugar according to the tartness of the fruit. Do not add lemon when using gooseberries.

Serve with softly whipped cream, Custard Sauce (page 93), or vanilla ice cream.

As directed beginning on page 10, prepare the pastry, roll out half of it, line a 9-inch pie pan, and partially bake; reserve the remaining pastry for the top crust. Cool the pie shell about 15 minutes before filling.

Preheat an oven to 425° F.

In a large bowl, toss the blueberries with the sugar, flour, nutmeg, cinnamon, and lemon zest and juice. Transfer to the pie crust, mounding the mixture slightly in the center. Dot with the butter.

Roll out the remaining pastry into a circle about ¹⁄₁₆ inch thick. Using a ruler as straight edge, cut the dough into strips about ½ inch wide with a sharp knife or rolling fluted pastry cutter. Arrange the strips in swirls as shown or as desired on top of the filling. Moisten the end of each strip with beaten egg white and press it to the pie shell. Top with a bow tied from one of the strips, if desired. Brush the pastry with the egg glaze and sprinkle with sugar. Cover the rim of the pie with aluminum foil strips to prevent overbrowning.

Bake for 25 minutes. Reduce the oven temperature to 350° F and cook until golden brown, about 30 minutes longer. Transfer to a wire rack to cool. Serve warm or at room temperature.

**Makes one 9-inch pie; serves 6 to 8.**

# Cherry Cream Pie

This old recipe is one of the best from my Grandmother Keith's kitchen in Jackson, Mississippi.

The crust can be cooked several hours ahead of time but is crispier when filled no longer than an hour before serving. When fresh cherries are unavailable, use frozen or canned cherries, or substitute a 1-pound can of cherry pie filling for the poached cherries. While light cream or half-and-half could be used in the stirred custard, evaporated milk adds a nice slightly caramelized flavor.

The top can be covered with meringue and browned, or with whipped cream instead of the fresh cherries and mint.

As directed beginning on page 10, prepare the pastry, roll out half of it, and line a 9-inch pie pan. Roll out the remaining pastry and cut with a small cookie cutter into rounds about the size of cherries. Moisten the rim of the pie shell with water and position the small rounds to encircle the pie. Bake completely. While the crust bakes, place any remaining rounds of pastry on a baking sheet and cook until golden; remove and reserve. Cool the pie shell completely before filling.

To poach the cherries, combine the water and cornstarch in a saucepan and bring to boil over high heat. Add the cherries, reduce the heat to low, and simmer until the cherries are tender. A couple of minutes before the cherries are cooked, stir in sugar according to the tartness of the cherries. Remove from the heat and reserve.

To make the custard filling, combine the egg yolks, sugar, cornstarch, and salt in a heavy saucepan and mix thoroughly. Slowly whisk or stir in the milk and cook over medium heat, stirring almost constantly, until the mixture thickens, about 8 to 10 minutes. Reduce the heat to very low and cook until quite thick, 3 or 4 minutes longer. Remove from the heat, add the butter, and stir until the butter melts. Stir in the vanilla and the cherry mixture. Transfer to a bowl, cover with plastic wrap laid directly on the surface of the custard, and let stand until cool, about 15 minutes.

Pour the filling into the cooled cooked pie crust and top with rounds of cooked pastry and fresh cherries and mint leaves, if available. Serve warm or at room temperature.

**Makes one 9-inch pie; serves 6 to 8.**

½ recipe Basic Pie Crust (page 10)

### POACHED CHERRIES
½ cup cold water
2 tablespoons cornstarch
2 cups stemmed and pitted fresh sweet Bing or Queen Anne cherries
¼ to ½ cup granulated sugar

### CUSTARD
3 egg yolks, lightly beaten
1 cup granulated sugar
¼ cup cornstarch
⅛ teaspoon salt
2 cups evaporated milk
2 tablespoons unsalted butter
1 teaspoon vanilla extract

Whole fresh cherries for garnish (optional)
Fresh mint leaves for garnish (optional)

# Summer Peach Pie

Basic Pie Crust (page 10)
4½ cups peeled, pitted, and sliced
   peaches (about 5 large)
1 cup granulated sugar
⅓ cup unbleached all-purpose flour
½ teaspoon ground cinnamon
   or ginger
2 tablespoons unsalted butter,
   cut into small pieces
1 egg white, lightly beaten
1 egg lightly beaten with 2 tablespoons
   heavy (whipping) cream for
   glazing
Granulated sugar for sprinkling

**When available, try Babcock, Strawberry Nectar, or other white peaches, or make the pie with nectarines. Serve with vanilla or ginger ice cream or Custard Sauce (page 93).**

As directed beginning on page 10, prepare the pastry, roll out half of it, line a 9-inch pie pan, and partially bake; reserve the remaining pastry for the top crust. Cool the pie shell about 15 minutes before filling.

Preheat an oven to 425° F.

In a bowl, combine the peaches, sugar, flour, and cinnamon or ginger and toss to coat the peaches well. Fill the cooled pie shell and dot with the butter.

Roll out the remaining pastry into a circle about ¹⁄₁₆ inch thick. Using another pie plate as a guide, cut the dough into a disk slightly larger than the diameter of the pie including the rim. Moisten the edges of the pie shell with the beaten egg white. Cut the top crust into wedges, and position the wedges slightly overlapping on top of the peaches. Fold back the points to reveal an opening at the center of the pie. Press the edges of the top and the bottom crust together; pinch off any excess dough and smooth the edges with your fingers. Brush the pastry with the egg glaze and sprinkle with sugar.

Bake for 15 minutes. Reduce the heat to 350° F and bake until golden brown, about 30 minutes longer. Remove to a wire rack to cool. Serve warm or at room temperature.

**Makes one 9-inch pie; serves 6 to 8.**

**VARIATION:** For a single-crust pie with a slightly crunchy top, fill a partially baked crust with peach slices or halves (cut side up). Combine 1 cup sugar, ½ cup flour, 1½ teaspoons cinnamon, and 1 cup heavy cream, mix well, and pour over the peaches. Bake in a preheated 425° F oven for 15 minutes, reduce heat to 300° F, and bake until the juices are bubbly and the top is lightly browned, about 45 to 50 minutes.

# Fresh Fig and Thyme Pie

**This unusual marriage of summer garden flavors creates pure magic.**

As directed beginning on page 10, prepare the pastry, roll out half of it, line a 9-inch pie pan, and partially bake; reserve the remaining pastry for the top crust. Cool the pie shell for about 15 minutes before filling.

Preheat an oven to 425° F.

In a bowl, toss the figs with the sugar, flour, thyme, and lemon juice. Transfer to the pie crust, mounding the mixture slightly in the center. Dot with butter.

Roll out the remaining pastry to a circle about 1/16 inch thick. Using another pie pan as a guide, cut a disk slightly larger than the top of the pie, including the rim. Moisten the edges of the pie shell with beaten egg white and cover the pie with the top crust. Press the edges of the top and bottom crusts together; pinch off any excess dough and smooth the edges with your fingers. Cut air vent holes and brush the crust with the egg glaze and sprinkle with sugar.

Bake for 15 minutes. Reduce the oven temperature to 350° F and cook until golden brown, about 45 minutes longer. Serve warm or at room temperature.

**Makes one 9-inch pie; serves 6 to 8.**

Basic Pie Crust (page 10)
5 cups stemmed and quartered fresh figs (about 40 medium-sized figs)
3/4 cup granulated sugar
6 tablespoons all-purpose flour, preferably unbleached
1 tablespoon fresh thyme leaves
2 tablespoons freshly squeezed lemon juice
2 tablespoons unsalted butter, cut into small pieces
1 egg white, lightly beaten
1 egg lightly beaten with 2 tablespoons heavy (whipping) cream for glazing
Granulated sugar for sprinkling

# Deep-Dish Fruit Pie

½ recipe Basic Pie Crust (page 10)
¾ cup granulated sugar, or to taste
¼ cup firmly packed light brown
　sugar
½ cup all-purpose flour, preferably
　unbleached
¾ teaspoon salt
1 teaspoon ground cinnamon, ginger,
　or cardamom, or freshly grated
　nutmeg
10 cups sliced fruit or whole berries
¼ cup freshly squeezed lemon juice
4 tablespoons (½ stick) unsalted
　butter, cut into small pieces
1 egg lightly beaten with 2 tablespoons
　heavy (whipping) cream for
　glazing
Granulated sugar for sprinkling

Since a deep-dish pie has no bottom crust to get soggy, it's a good choice for a pie that cannot be served immediately. Choose a baking dish that is about 3 inches deep and fill with any berries or fruit that are in seasonal abundance. Peel and core apples or pears before slicing them; peel and pit apricots, nectarines, or peaches. Adjust the amount of sugar and lemon juice to the natural sweetness of the fruit and vary the spices to suit the fruit. Cinnamon and/or nutmeg highlights any fruit, but is especially good with apples or pears, ginger complements peaches or apricots, and cardamom transforms familiar fruits into exotic flavors.

**To make individual pies, as shown, divide the mixture among small ovenproof shallow bowls. Serve the pie warm and offer a pitcher of heavy cream for drizzling over the top.**

As directed beginning on page 10, prepare the pastry, roll out to fit the top of the baking dish with about a 1-inch overhang, place on a baking sheet, cover with waxed paper, and refrigerate until needed.

Preheat an oven to 425° F.

In a mixing bowl, combine the sugars, flour, salt, and cinnamon and stir to mix well.

In a large bowl, toss the fruit with the lemon juice. Add the dry mixture and toss to coat evenly. Pour into a baking pan (see recipe introduction) and dot with the butter. Cover with the reserved pastry, fold the overhang under itself to make a double-thick rim around the edge of the dish, and crimp the edges to form an attractive border. Use a sharp knife to cut several steam vents. Brush the top with the egg glaze and sprinkle with sugar.

Bake for 25 minutes, then reduce the temperature to 350° F and bake until the fruit is tender when pierced with a skewer and the crust is golden brown, about 25 minutes longer. Remove to a wire rack and cool for about 15 minutes or to room temperature.

**Makes one 9-inch pie; serves 6 to 8.**

# Apple Orchard Pie

Although there are countless versions of apple pie, I think that simplicity is best. My preference leans to thinly sliced flavorful apples such as Cortland, Gravenstein, Granny Smith, or Winesap. You may need to add a bit more sugar if the apples are very tart. This country-style pie is made without any thickener, so don't expect neat slices of pie. If you prefer a firmer filling, mix about 3 tablespoons flour with the sugar. The Cheddar Crust on page 11 adds a new dimension.

It's hard to beat warm apple pie with a scoop of good vanilla ice cream, but a drizzle of Warm Cinnamon Cider Sauce (page 93) is a grand alternative or addition. Try firm ripe pears as an alternative.

As directed beginning on page 10, prepare the pastry, roll out half of it, line a 9-inch pie pan, and partially bake; reserve the remaining pastry for the top crust. Cool the pie shell about 15 minutes before filling.

Preheat an oven to 425° F.

In a large bowl, combine the sugar, salt, cinnamon, and cloves and mix well. Add the apples and toss to thoroughly coat the slices with the dry ingredients. Sprinkle with the lemon juice and zest and toss to blend. Turn the apples into the cooled shell, mounding them slightly in the center. Dot with the butter.

Roll out the remaining pastry to a circle about 1/16 inch thick. Using another pie pan as a guide, cut a disk slightly larger than the top of the pie, including the rim. Moisten the edges of the pie shell with beaten egg white and cover the pie with the top crust. Press the edges of the top and bottom crusts together; pinch off any excess dough and smooth the edges with your fingers. Cut air vent holes and brush the pastry with the egg glaze. Decorate top if desired with cutouts made from pastry scraps and brush them with the egg glaze and sprinkle with sugar.

Bake for 10 minutes. Reduce the heat to 350° F and cook until the crust is golden brown, about 40 minutes longer. Transfer to a wire rack to cool. Serve slightly warm.

**Makes one 9-inch pie; serves 6 to 8.**

Basic Pie Crust (page 10), preferably made with shortening or lard
¾ cup granulated sugar, or to taste
¼ teaspoon salt
¾ teaspoon ground cinnamon
⅛ teaspoon ground cloves
8 cups peeled, cored, and thinly sliced crisp apples (about 3 pounds)
1 tablespoon freshly squeezed lemon juice
1 teaspoon grated or minced lemon zest
4 tablespoons (¼ stick) unsalted butter, cut into small pieces
1 egg white, lightly beaten
1 egg yolk lightly beaten with 2 tablespoons heavy (whipping) cream for glazing
Granulated sugar for sprinkling

# Cranberry Orange Pie

Basic Pie Crust (page 10)
3½ cups fresh cranberries (about
    1 package)
1 cup granulated sugar
1½ tablespoons all-purpose flour,
    preferably unbleached
¼ teaspoon salt
3 tablespoons freshly squeezed
    orange juice
2 tablespoons minced or grated
    orange zest
2 tablespoons unsalted butter,
    melted
1 egg, lightly beaten
1 egg lightly beaten with 2 tablespoons
    heavy (whipping) cream for
    glazing
Granulated sugar for sprinkling

After a big rich Thanksgiving feast, this slightly tart pie, a variation on an old Cape Cod recipe, is welcomed and offers a different way of adding the traditional berries to the menu. However, the pie is so good that you'll want to freeze several bags of berries during season to enjoy it more than once a year.

As directed beginning on page 10, prepare the pastry, roll out half of it, line a 9-inch pie pan, and partially bake; reserve the remaining pastry for the top crust. Cool the pie shell about 15 minutes before filling.

Preheat an oven to 450° F.

In a large bowl, combine the cranberries, sugar, flour, salt, orange juice and zest, and melted butter and toss to blend well. Pour into the cooled pie shell.

Roll out the remaining pastry to a circle about ⅟₁₆ inch thick. Using a ruler as a straight edge, cut with a sharp knife or rolling pastry cutter into strips about ½ inch wide. Moisten the edges of the pie shell with beaten egg and criss-cross the dough strips to form a lattice design over the cranberries. Press the edges of the top and bottom crusts together; pinch off any excess dough and smooth the edges with your fingers. Brush the top of the pastry with egg glaze and sprinkle with sugar.

Bake for 10 minutes. Reduce the heat to 350° F and bake until the crust is golden brown and the juices are bubbly, about 45 minutes longer.

**Makes one 9-inch pie; serves 6 to 8.**

# Sweet Potato Pie

½ recipe Basic Pie Crust (page 10),
    preferably made with shortening
    or lard
1¼ pounds yams or sweet potatoes
    (about 2 medium-sized)
1 cup granulated sugar
½ teaspoon salt
¼ teaspoon baking soda
½ teaspoon ground cinnamon
¼ teaspoon freshly grated nutmeg
¼ teaspoon ground cloves
¼ cup (½ stick) unsalted butter,
    melted
1 teaspoon vanilla extract
2 eggs
½ cup milk

**Matilda Adams in my hometown of Jonesville, Louisiana, made the best sweet potato pie I've ever tasted. In spite of the name, the pie is more flavorful when made with sweet potato's deeper-colored cousin, the yam.**

As directed beginning on page 10, prepare the pastry, roll out, line a 9-inch pie pan, and partially bake. Cool the pie shell about 15 minutes before filling.

Scrub the skin of the yams or sweet potatoes to remove any dirt. Place them in a large saucepan and add enough cold water to cover. Bring to a boil over medium-high heat and cook until almost tender, about 35 to 40 minutes. Drain and let stand until cool enough to handle, then peel and cut into chunks. Alternatively, the yams or sweet potatoes can be steamed, baked, or microwaved. Mash through a potato ricer or with a potato masher; food processors make them too smooth.

Preheat an oven to 375° F.

In a large bowl, mix the mashed yams or sweet potatoes with the sugar, salt, baking soda, cinnamon, nutmeg, and cloves. Beat in the melted butter, vanilla extract, eggs, and milk. Pour the mixture into the pie shell and cover the rim of pastry with aluminum foil strips to prevent overbrowning.

Bake until the top feels just firm to the touch and just begins to brown, about 40 minutes. Transfer to a wire rack to cool to room temperature before serving.

**Makes one 9-inch pie; serves 6 to 8.**

# Winter Squash Pie

Butternut, buttercup, sugar pumpkin, or other flavorful winter squash varieties make pie with a taste that is superior to their field pumpkin relative. When you're in a hurry or fresh squash is unavailable, canned pumpkin purée (not pie filling mix) can be substituted.

As directed beginning on page 10, prepare the pastry, roll out half of it, line a 9-inch pie pan, and partially bake; reserve the remaining pastry for the top crust. Cool the pie shell about 15 minutes before filling.

To make the top crust design shown here, pinch off a piece of the remaining pastry and roll it out with your hands to form a rope about 6 inches long and ½ inch in diameter at one end and tapering to a point on the other end. Place on a cookie sheet and bend slightly in several places to resemble a tree branch. Roll out the remaining pastry and cut with leaf-shaped cookie cutters or cut out leaf shapes with a sharp knife; arrange on the cookie sheet, cover with plastic wrap, and reserve. Alternatively, the top of the pie can be decorated with other cookie shapes or left unadorned (in which case you'll only need ½ recipe of pastry).

Preheat an oven to 375° F.

In a large bowl, combine the puréed squash, salt, cinnamon, ginger, syrup, eggs, cream, and vanilla and beat well. Pour the mixture into the cooled pie shell and cover the rim of the pastry with aluminum foil strips to prevent overbrowning.

Bake until a knife inserted in the center comes out clean, about 1 hour. Transfer to a wire rack to cool to room temperature.

Meanwhile, brush the pastry leaves and branch, if using, with beaten egg and sprinkle the branch with the cinnamon-sugar. Bake until golden, about 15 minutes for the leaves, and about 25 minutes for the branch. Transfer to a wire rack to cool before arranging on top of the cooled pie.

**Makes one 9-inch pie; serves 6 to 8.**

Basic Pie Crust (page 10), made with brown sugar and cinnamon (page 11)
1½ cups puréed baked winter squash
1 teaspoon salt
1 teaspoon ground cinnamon
1 teaspoon ground ginger
⅔ cup maple syrup or packed brown sugar
4 eggs, lightly beaten
1 cup heavy (whipping) cream, light cream, or half-and-half
1 teaspoon vanilla extract
1 egg, lightly beaten
1 tablespoon brown sugar mixed with 1 teaspoon ground cinnamon

# Sesame Walnut Pie

**A California combination that calls for a scoop of rich coffee ice cream.**

As directed beginning on page 10, prepare the pastry, line a 9-inch pie pan, and partially bake. Cool the pie shell about 15 minutes before filling.

Preheat an oven to 350° F.

Combine the eggs, sugar, and salt in a large bowl and beat until well mixed. Blend in the syrup, butter, and vanilla. Stir in the walnuts and sesame seeds. Pour into the pie shell and cover the rim of the pastry with aluminum foil strips to prevent overbrowning.

Bake until a knife inserted into the center tests barely clean, about 50 minutes; do not overcook. Transfer to a wire rack and cool. Serve warm or at room temperature.

**Makes one 9-inch pie; serves 6 to 8.**

½ recipe Basic Pie Crust (page 10)
3 eggs, lightly beaten
1 cup firmly packed dark brown sugar
½ teaspoon salt
1 cup dark corn syrup
4 tablespoons (½ stick) unsalted
    butter, melted and cooled
1 teaspoon vanilla extract
1 cup chopped walnuts
1 cup sesame seeds

# Southern Pecan Pie

½ recipe Basic Pie Crust (page 10)
3 eggs, lightly beaten
⅔ cup granulated sugar
1 tablespoon all-purpose flour,
    preferably unbleached
¼ teaspoon salt
1 cup light corn syrup
4 tablespoons (½ stick) unsalted
    butter, melted
1 teaspoon vanilla extract
1 cup chopped pecans
1 cup pecan halves

Many pecan pies are too sticky sweet for my taste. This lighter version was taught to me years ago by my fifth-grade teacher, Eula Cain, and makes regular appearances at my winter holiday festivities.

If you prefer a darker, heavier pie, substitute brown sugar for the granulated and use dark corn syrup or half molasses and half corn syrup. Although good alone, the dense pie is even better with a dollop of softly whipped cream flavored to taste with bourbon or vanilla extract.

As directed beginning on page 10, prepare the pastry, line a 9-inch pie pan, and bake completely. Cool the pie shell about 15 minutes before filling.

Preheat an oven to 375° F.

Combine the eggs, sugar, flour, salt, syrup, butter, and vanilla in a large bowl and beat until well blended. Stir in the chopped pecans and pour into the cooled pie shell. Arrange the pecan halves on top of the mixture. Cover the rim of the pie shell with foil to prevent overbrowning.

Bake until the edges of the pie feel set when touched but the center still jiggles slightly, about 50 minutes. The filling should remain just a bit gooey but not syrupy, and a knife inserted into the center should still have tracings of filling when removed. Transfer to a wire rack to cool. Serve warm or at room temperature.

**Makes one 9-inch pie; serves 6 to 8.**

**VARIATIONS:** Substitute walnuts, macadamias, peanuts, or an array of mixed nuts for the pecans.

# Hazelnut Chocolate Pie

½ recipe Basic Pie Crust (page 10),
    preferably Chocolate Variation
    (page 11)
3 eggs
¾ cup granulated sugar
¼ teaspoon salt
1½ cups hazelnuts (filberts),
    finely chopped
6 ounces bittersweet or semisweet
    chocolate, coarsely chopped

DARK CHOCOLATE GLAZE
    (optional)
4 ounces bittersweet or semisweet
    chocolate, finely chopped
2 tablespoons heavy (whipping)
    cream
1½ tablespoons unsalted butter

WHITE CHOCOLATE GLAZE
    (optional)
4 ounces white chocolate, finely
    chopped
2 tablespoons heavy (whipping)
    cream
1½ tablespoons unsalted butter

The classic Italian blend of hazelnuts with chocolate is heaven-sent, but almonds, macadamias, walnuts, or pecans could be used in this super-rich confection.

If you wish to remove the husks from the hazelnuts, drop whole nuts into boiling water for about a minute. Drain and pour the nuts onto a clean cloth towel and rub them with the towel while still warm to remove as much of the husks as possible; don't worry about areas that will not come off easily.

As directed beginning on page 10, prepare the pastry, line a 9-inch pie pan, and partially bake. Cool the pie shell about 15 minutes before filling.

Preheat an oven to 350° F.

Combine the eggs, sugar, and salt in a mixing bowl and beat until thick. Add the hazelnuts and the chocolate and blend well. Pour into the pie shell and cover the rim of the pastry with aluminum foil strips to prevent overbrowning.

Bake until a knife inserted in the center tests slightly gooey, about 40 to 45 minutes. Cool completely before adding glaze.

To make the optional glazes, place each chocolate and cream in separate bowls and microwave, stirring frequently, until melted, about 1 minute. Alternatively, set in separate containers over barely simmering water and stir gently until the chocolate melts. Remove from the microwave or heat and gently whisk in the butter until melted. Cool slightly, then transfer to a pastry bag fitted with a small plain tip or a plastic bag with a small hole cut in one corner. Pipe the glaze over the pie as desired. Let stand until set.

Serve the pie at room temperature.

**Makes one 9-inch pie; serves 6 to 8.**

# Citrus Cream Pie

Any citrus fruit can be used to make the smooth, rich filling for this pie. Adjust the amount of sugar to suit your taste and the acidity of the fruit, a bit more for lime and less for oranges or tangerines.

To make the filling, beat the egg yolks and whole eggs together in the top container of a double boiler. Stir in the sugar, citrus juice and zest and place over simmering water. Add the butter, 1 tablespoon at a time, and stir constantly until each piece of butter melts and the mixture thickens to a custard consistency, about 20 minutes. Remove from the heat and place a piece of plastic wrap directly on the surface of the filling. Cool to room temperature, then refrigerate until well chilled; can be stored up to 1 month.

As directed beginning on page 10 or 91, prepare the pastry, roll out, line a 9-inch pie pan, and bake completely. Cool the pie shell for about 15 minutes before filling.

To assemble the pie, pour the cream into a well-chilled bowl and whip until firm peaks form. Stir about one third of the cream into the citrus filling to lighten it, then fold in the remaining cream. Pour into the cooled pastry shell. Refrigerate until well chilled, about 2 to 3 hours.

Garnish with candied citrus zest just before serving, if desired.

**Makes one 9-inch pie; serves 6 to 8.**

NOTE: To make candied citrus zest, cut the thin colored layer from 1 or 2 fruits into julienne. Bring 1 cup sugar and ¼ cup water to a boil over medium heat, reduce the heat to low, add the citrus zest, and simmer for about 15 minutes. Remove the strips to a wire rack to cool. Roll the strips in granulated sugar to coat. Store in tightly covered containers for up to 1 week at room temperature.

**CITRUS FILLING**
2 egg yolks
4 eggs
1⅓ cups granulated sugar, or to taste
½ cup freshly squeezed citrus juice
1 to 2 tablespoons grated or minced citrus zest (same type as juice)
½ cup (1 stick) unsalted butter, cut into small pieces

½ recipe Basic Pie Crust (page 10), or 1 recipe Coconut Crust (page 91)
1½ cups heavy (whipping) cream
Candied citrus zest (see note; optional)

# Key Lime Pie

½ recipe Basic Pie Crust (page 10)
4 egg yolks
1 can (14 ounces) sweetened
    condensed milk
½ cup or more freshly squeezed
    lime juice
1 tablespoon grated lime zest
    (optional)
1 cup heavy (whipping) cream
3 tablespoons powdered sugar
Grated lime zest for sprinkling
    (optional)

This Florida classic originated with the tart juice of the small round yellowish Mexican Caribbean limes that grow in the Keys. More readily available Persian limes also create a delicious filling.

Some people prefer filling a Cookie Crumb Crust (page 90) made with graham crackers. Others like to finish the pie with Meringue Topping (page 92). Any combination is delicious.

**Substitute lemon juice to make the old favorite, Lemon Ice Box Pie.**

As directed beginning on page 10, prepare the pastry, roll out, line a 9-inch pie pan, and bake completely. Cool the pie shell for about 15 minutes before filling.

Preheat an oven to 350° F.

Beat the egg yolks in a large bowl. Add the condensed milk, and lime juice and zest, if using. Taste and add more lime juice if required to create a tart flavor. Pour the mixture into the cooled shell and bake 15 minutes. Cool to room temperature.

Whip the cream, adding the sugar 1 tablespoon at a time, until it holds its shape. Spoon over the top of the pie, or transfer to a pastry bag and pipe over the top of the cooled pie in a fanciful pattern. Sprinkle with the lime zest, if using. Serve at room temperature.

**Makes one 9-inch pie; serves 6 to 8.**

VARIATION: For a fluffy filling, prepare as directed, using only 3 egg yolks. Before pouring into the shell, fold in 3 egg whites, beaten until stiff but not dry.

# Lemon Meringue Pie

I've always been disappointed in gluelike commercial renditions of this American treasure. Here is my mother's version, which we always ate still a little warm.

As directed beginning on page 10, prepare the pastry, roll out, line a 9-inch pie pan, and bake completely. Cool the pie shell about 15 minutes before filling.

In a heavy saucepan, combine the cornstarch, sugar, and salt. Gradually stir in the cold water and lemon juice, then the boiling water. Place over medium-low heat and bring the mixture to a boil, stirring constantly to prevent lumps. Cook until thick, about 5 minutes. Remove from the heat, add the butter, and stir until the butter melts.

Beat the egg yolks in a small heatproof bowl. Slowly beat in about ¼ cup of the cornstarch mixture. Return this mixture to the mixture in the pan. Stir in the lemon zest. Return to the heat and cook until thickened, about 1 minute longer. Remove from heat and let cool about 15 minutes.

Preheat an oven to 350° F.

Pour the filling into the cooled pie shell. Top with meringue as described on page 92 and bake until lightly browned. Transfer to a wire rack to cool. Serve slightly warm or at room temperature.

**Makes one 9-inch pie; serves 6 to 8.**

½ recipe Basic Pie Crust (page 10)
6 tablespoons cornstarch
1½ cups granulated sugar
¼ teaspoon salt
½ cup cold water
½ cup freshly squeezed lemon juice
1½ cups boiling water
3 tablespoons unsalted butter,
    at room temperature
3 egg yolks (reserve whites
    for topping)
2 teaspoons grated or minced
    lemon zest
Meringue Topping (page 92)

# Lemon Slice Pie

Basic Pie Crust (page 10)
1½ cups granulated sugar
2 tablespoons all-purpose flour,
    preferably unbleached
¼ teaspoon salt
4 tablespoons (½ stick) unsalted
    butter, melted
3 eggs, well beaten
¼ cup water
¼ cup freshly squeezed lemon juice
3 large thin-skinned lemons,
    preferably peeled, sliced as thinly
    as possible, and seeded
1 egg white, lightly beaten,
1 egg lightly beaten with 2 tablespoons
    heavy (whipping) cream for
    glazing
Powdered sugar

**I adore the tartness of this variation on a Shaker tradition, especially when made with 'Meyer' variety lemons. Any lemons with very thin skins do not require peeling, although I prefer the texture of the pie when the lemons have been peeled. My friend Marian May suggests peeling the lemons, removing all white pith, and freezing them in plastic bags to facilitate slicing them thinly.**

As directed, beginning on page 10, prepare the pastry, roll out half of it, line a 9-inch pie pan, and partially bake; reserve the remaining pastry for the top crust. Cool the pie shell about 15 minutes before filling.

Preheat an oven to 425° F.

In a large bowl, combine the sugar, flour, and salt. Beat in the butter and eggs. Stir in the water, lemon juice, and lemon slices. Pour into the pie shell.

Roll out the remaining pastry to a circle about ¹⁄₁₆ inch thick. Using another pie pan as a guide, cut a disk slightly larger than the top of the pie, including the rim. Moisten the edges of the pie shell with beaten egg white and cover the pie with the top crust. Press the edges of the top and bottom crusts together; pinch off any excess dough and smooth the edges with your fingers. Cut air vent holes and brush the pastry with the egg glaze. Decorate the top or the rim as desired with cutouts made from pastry scraps and brush them with egg glaze.

Bake 15 minutes. Reduce the oven temperature to 350° F and cook until the crust is golden brown, about 25 minutes longer. Cover rim with foil strips if it begins to get too brown. Transfer to a wire rack to cool to room temperature. Dust with powdered sugar before serving.

**Makes one 9-inch pie; serves 6 to 8.**

# Coconut-Coconut-Coconut Pie

**Rich coconut milk is used to make the stirred coconut custard, and shredded coconut appears in the chewy crust and is sprinkled over the meringue topping. Although freshly shredded coconut is naturally best, packaged coconut makes an acceptable substitute.**

Prepare the crust as directed on page 91. Cool completely before filling.

In a heavy saucepan, combine the egg yolks, sugar, cornstarch, and salt and mix thoroughly. Slowly whisk or stir in the coconut milk or milk and cook over medium heat, stirring and scraping the bottom constantly, until the mixture thickens, about 8 to 10 minutes. Reduce the heat to very low and cook until quite thick, 3 or 4 minutes longer. Remove from the heat, add the butter, and stir until the butter melts. If made with coconut milk, stir in the vanilla; if made with milk, stir in the coconut extract. Transfer to a bowl, cover with plastic wrap laid directly on the surface of the custard and let stand until cool, about 15 minutes.

Preheat an oven to 350° F.

Pour the filling into the cooled crust. Cover with the meringue topping, sprinkle with coconut, and bake until lightly browned, about 10 to 15 minutes. Transfer to a wire rack and cool to room temperature. Serve at room temperature. Refrigerate if it will be more than 1 hour before serving; remove from the refrigerator at least 30 minutes before serving.

**Makes one 9-inch pie; serves 6 to 8.**

**VARIATION:** For traditional Coconut Cream Pie, prepare ½ recipe Basic Pie Crust (page 10) and bake completely. Make the custard with regular milk and stir in 1¼ cups shredded coconut along with the vanilla extract.

Coconut Crust (page 91)

COCONUT CUSTARD
4 egg yolks, lightly beaten
    (reserve whites for topping)
¾ cup granulated sugar
¼ cup cornstarch
⅛ teaspoon salt
2½ cups canned unsweetened coconut
    milk (available in Asian markets)
    or milk
4 tablespoons (½ stick) unsalted
    butter, at room temperature
2 teaspoons vanilla or coconut extract

Meringue Topping (page 92)
Shredded fresh or dried coconut
    for sprinkling

# Tropical Fruit Macadamia Pie

Nut Crust (page 91), made with
    macadamia nuts
4 egg yolks, lightly beaten
¾ cup granulated sugar
¼ cup cornstarch
¼ teaspoon salt
2¾ cups milk
2 cups chopped fresh mango, papaya,
    or pineapple or drained canned
    crushed pineapple
4 tablespoons (½ stick) unsalted
    butter, at room temperature
2 tablespoons light rum, or
    2 teaspoons vanilla extract
Chopped macadamia nuts for garnish

One taste of this tropical combo transports you to Hawaii. Stir either ripe mango, papaya, pineapple, or a combination into the smooth custard. When fresh fruits are not available, drained canned crushed pineapple is an acceptable alternative.

To create the tropical sunset pattern shown here, divide the slightly thickened custard into one-third and two-thirds portions. Stir puréed papaya or mango into the smaller portion and puréed or crushed pineapple into the larger portion. Complete the custard and cool, then pour the pineapple custard into the pie shell, spoon the other mixture into the center, and pull a spatula or dull knife blade through to spread the mixture into the pineapple custard.

**Serve with softly whipped cream flavored with a bit of rum, if desired.**

Prepare the Nut Crust as directed on page 91. Bake and cool completely before filling.

In a heavy saucepan, combine the egg yolks, sugar, cornstarch, and salt and mix thoroughly. Slowly whisk or stir in the milk and cook over medium heat, stirring constantly, until the mixture thickens, about 8 to 10 minutes. Stir in the fruit, reduce the heat to very low, and cook until quite thick, 3 or 4 minutes longer. Remove from the heat, add butter, and stir until the butter melts. Stir in the rum or vanilla. Transfer to a bowl, cover with plastic wrap laid directly on the surface of the custard, and let stand until cool.

Pour the filling into the cooled crust. Garnish with chopped macadamia nuts.

**Makes one 9-inch pie; serves 6 to 8.**

# Banana Pudding Pie

Cookie Crumb Crust (page 90),
    made with vanilla wafers

VANILLA CUSTARD
3 egg yolks, lightly beaten
½ cup granulated sugar
6 tablespoons cornstarch
¼ teaspoon salt
2½ cups light cream or half-and-half
2 tablespoons unsalted butter,
    at room temperature
1 teaspoon vanilla extract

3 medium-sized ripe bananas
Meringue Topping (page 92)

My mouth waters when I remember my Grandmother Izetta McNair's banana pudding. For an unexpected treat, I've turned the ingredients into a pie. Substitute a fully baked Basic Pie Crust (page 10) for the vanilla wafer crust and top with sweetened whipped cream instead of meringue and you'll have an American classic: Banana Cream Pie.

**Sweet and creamy red bananas make an exceptional filling.**

As directed on page 90, prepare the crumb crust and line a 9-inch pie pan. Bake and cool or chill to set before filling.

To make the vanilla custard, combine the egg yolks, sugar, cornstarch, and salt in a heavy saucepan. Whisk or stir in the light cream or half-and-half and cook over medium heat, stirring and scraping the bottom constantly, until the mixture thickens, about 8 to 10 minutes. Reduce the heat to very low and cook until quite thick, 3 or 4 minutes longer. Remove from the heat, add the butter and vanilla, and stir until the butter melts. Transfer to a bowl, cover with plastic wrap placed directly on the surface of the custard, and cool to room temperature.

To assemble the pie, peel and slice the bananas. Spread one third of the custard in the pie shell and cover with half of the bananas. Top with half of the remaining custard, then the remaining bananas. Cover with the remaining custard.

Preheat an oven to 350° F.

Prepare the Meringue Topping as described on page 92 and cover the top of the pie. Bake until golden brown, about 10 to 15 minutes. Transfer to a wire rack to cool to room temperature before serving.

**Makes one 9-inch pie; serves 6 to 8.**

# STAPLE PIES

Here are a dozen scrumptious pies that do not rely on seasonal availability. Most are made from ingredients that are usually on hand in the refrigerator or pantry: buttermilk, cream, chocolate, coffee, sugar, dried fruit, peanut butter, and even crackers. Enjoy them all year round.

# Early American Buttermilk Pie

**This comforting old favorite is a perfect light ending to a heavy meal. I especially enjoy it with a sprinkling of just-warmed blueberries.**

As directed beginning on page 10, prepare the pastry, roll it out, line a 9-inch pie pan, and partially bake. Cool the pie shell about 15 minutes before filling.

Preheat an oven to 350° F.

In a large bowl, stir the sugar, flour, salt, and nutmeg together. Using a wire whisk or wooden spoon, blend in the eggs. Add the buttermilk and vanilla and beat until smooth. Pour into the cooled pie shell and cover the rim of the pastry with aluminum foil strips to prevent overbrowning.

Bake until a knife inserted into the center comes out barely clean, about 45 to 55 minutes. Transfer to a wire rack and cool to room temperature.

**Makes one 9-inch pie; serves 6 to 8.**

½ recipe Basic Pie Crust (page 10)
1 cup granulated sugar
¼ cup all-purpose flour, preferably
    unbleached
½ teaspoon salt
⅛ teaspoon freshly grated nutmeg
4 eggs, lightly beaten
2 cups buttermilk
1 teaspoon vanilla extract

# Ginger Crème Brûlée Pie

**I first encountered a similar pie several years ago at a trendy San Francisco diner.**

As directed beginning on page 10, prepare the pastry, roll it out, line a 9-inch pie pan, and partially bake. Cool the pie shell about 15 minutes before filling.

Combine the ginger and cream in a saucepan over medium-low heat and simmer until the mixture comes almost to a boil.

Preheat an oven to 300° F.

In a large bowl, beat the egg yolks and sugar with a wire whisk. Gradually pour the hot cream through a fine wire sieve into the egg mixture and beat until smooth. Pour the mixture into the pie shell. Cover the pastry rim with foil to prevent overbrowning.

Bake until the custard is set and a knife inserted in the center comes out almost clean, about 1 hour. Remove from the oven and cool, then refrigerate for at least 1 hour or up to 3 hours.

About 30 minutes before serving, preheat the broiler.

Push the brown sugar through a sieve directly over the pie to form an even layer. Using a mister, spray the sugar with a little water. Heat under the broiler until the sugar melts and the top is bubbly, about 1 minute; watch carefully to prevent burning. Refrigerate just long enough for the melted sugar to form a crisp crust, about 20 minutes. Do not leave in the refrigerator too long or the crust will melt. Garnish with the preserved or crystalized ginger.

**Makes one 9-inch pie; serves 6 to 8.**

**VARIATION:** Omit ginger for traditional crème brûlée flavor.

½ recipe Basic Pie Crust (page 10)
2 tablespoons minced peeled fresh ginger root
3 cups heavy (whipping) cream
8 egg yolks
5 tablespoons granulated sugar
About ⅓ cup light brown sugar
Thinly sliced preserved or crystalized ginger for garnish

# Southern Chess Pie

This old treasure came to the southern colonies from England. Some folks say the name came from the melodic drawl, which turned the common name for this plain buttery pie, "just pie" into "jess pie." In fact, *cheese* was an old cooking term for curdling milk or thickening egg mixtures with heat.

As directed beginning on page 10, prepare the pastry, roll out, line a 9-inch pie pan, and bake partially. Cool the pie shell for about 15 minutes before filling.

Preheat an oven to 325° F.

In a large bowl, combine the egg yolks, whole egg, sugar, cornmeal, salt, and melted butter and beat well. Blend in the evaporated milk, cream, or half-and-half, lemon juice, and vanilla extract. Pour into the cooled pie shell.

Bake until the filling is set to the touch or a knife inserted 1 inch from the center comes out clean, about 40 minutes. Transfer to a wire rack and cool. Serve warm or at room temperature.

**Makes one 9-inch pie; serves 6 to 8.**

½ recipe Basic Pie Crust (page 10)
3 egg yolks
1 egg
1 cup granulated sugar
2 tablespoons yellow cornmeal
⅛ teaspoon salt
½ cup (1 stick) unsalted butter, melted
½ cup evaporated milk, heavy (whipping) cream, or half-and-half
1 tablespoon freshly squeezed lemon juice
2 teaspoons vanilla extract

# Mystery Pie

3 egg whites
1 cup granulated sugar
½ teaspoon baking powder
2 teaspoons vanilla extract
1 cup chopped pecans
20 Ritz crackers, finely crushed
1 cup heavy (whipping) cream
2 tablespoons powdered sugar,
  or to taste
3 tablespoons chopped fresh mint
  (optional)
Sliced oranges or kiwi fruit for
  garnish (optional)

**Ruth Dosher, one of the best cooks in my hometown, bakes this 1950s-style pie in which the meringue crust and the filling are combined. It was such a favorite of my daddy's, who was the Baptist minister, that it became known about town as "Preacher's Pie." Unless told, chances are that no one would guess the surprise ingredient to be Ritz crackers.**

Preheat an oven to 350° F.

In a large bowl, beat the egg whites until soft peaks form. Gradually beat in the sugar, baking powder, and 1 teaspoon of the vanilla, and continue beating until stiff but not dry. Fold in the pecans and cracker crumbs.

Pour the mixture into a buttered 9-inch pie pan and bake until set, about 30 minutes. Remove from the oven and cool on a wire rack to room temperature.

Cover with plastic wrap and refrigerate for at least 3 hours or as long as overnight.

Just before serving, whip the cream as directed on page 92, adding powdered sugar to taste, the remaining 1 teaspoon vanilla, and chopped mint, if desired. Spread over the chilled pie. Garnish with fruit slices, if using.

**Makes one 9-inch pie; serves 6 to 8.**

# Hot Chocolate Pie

I call this chocolate pie, which I most associate with my mother's kitchen, "hot" because I enjoy it best when it's still quite warm from the oven. If you prefer, substitute 3 ounces melted baking chocolate for the cocoa powder, adding it along with the butter.

Mother always covered her pie with meringue, but it is also good served with dollops of softly whipped cream. To make the meringue mounds shown here, prepare the topping, spoon it onto a greased cookie sheet, and bake. Transfer to the pie with a spatula and serve immediately.

As directed beginning on page 10, prepare the pastry, roll it out, line a 9-inch pie pan, and bake completely. Cool the pie shell about 15 minutes before filling.

In a heavy saucepan, combine the egg yolks, sugar, salt, flour, and cocoa powder and beat until smooth. Slowly whisk or stir in the milk and cook over medium heat, stirring constantly, until the mixture thickens, about 8 to 10 minutes. Reduce the heat to very low and cook until quite thick, 3 or 4 minutes longer. Remove from the heat, add the butter and stir until the butter melts. Stir in the vanilla. Transfer to a bowl, cover with plastic wrap laid directly on the surface of the custard, and let stand until slightly cool, about 10 minutes.

Preheat an oven to 350° F.

Pour the chocolate filling into the cooled pie shell and top with the meringue.

Bake until the meringue is lightly browned, 10 to 15 minutes. Transfer to a wire rack and cool. Serve warm or at room temperature.

**Makes one 9-inch pie; serves 6 to 8.**

½ recipe Basic Pie Crust (page 10)
4 egg yolks, lightly beaten
    (reserve whites for topping)
1 cup granulated sugar
½ teaspoon salt
5 tablespoons all-purpose flour,
    preferably unbleached
¼ cup unsweetened cocoa powder
2 cups milk
3 tablespoons unsalted butter
1½ teaspoons vanilla extract
Meringue Topping (page 92)

# Decadent Fudge Pie

½ cup Basic Pie Crust (page 10)
¾ cup (1½ sticks) unsalted butter
3 ounces (3 squares) unsweetened chocolate
3 eggs, at room temperature
1¾ cups granulated sugar
6 tablespoons all-purpose flour, preferably unbleached
¼ teaspoon salt
3 teaspoons vanilla extract

**Delicious on its own, but even better with Custard Sauce (page 93).**

As directed beginning on page 10, prepare the pastry, roll it out, line a 9-inch pie pan, and partially bake. Cool the pie shell about 15 minutes before filling.

Combine the butter and chocolate in a heavy saucepan over low heat and cook, stirring occasionally, until melted. Remove from heat to cool.

Preheat an oven to 350° F.

In a large bowl, lightly beat the eggs. Add the sugar, flour, and salt and beat until well blended. Add the cooled chocolate mixture and vanilla and stir until smooth. Pour into the cooled pie shell.

Bake until a knife inserted into the center remains a bit gooey, about 30 to 35 minutes. Transfer to a wire rack and cool to room temperature.

**Makes one 9-inch pie; serves 6 to 8.**

**VARIATION:** Add ½ cup finely chopped nuts to filling before pouring into crust.

# Three-Tone Chocolate Mousse Pie

Cookie Crumb Crust (page 90), made
  with chocolate wafers
½ cup heavy (whipping) cream
6 egg whites
3 tablespoons granulated sugar

DARK CHOCOLATE MOUSSE
5 ounces bittersweet or semisweet
  chocolate, finely chopped
4 tablespoons (½ stick) unsalted
  butter, at room temperature
2 egg yolks

MILK CHOCOLATE MOUSSE
5 ounces milk chocolate, finely
  chopped
4 tablespoons (½ stick) unsalted
  butter, at room temperature
2 egg yolks

WHITE CHOCOLATE MOUSSE
5 ounces white chocolate,
  finely chopped
4 tablespoons (½ stick) unsalted
  butter, at room temperature
2 egg yolks

Dark, milk, and white chocolate curls
  or other chocolate decorations
  (for garnish; optional)

Dark, milk, and white chocolate mousses turn this pie into a chocoholic's dream. Use the finest chocolate available, such as Callebaut, Lindt, or Tobler.

To make the arrow shown here, melt 2 ounces of dark chocolate in a microwave or over simmering water, stirring frequently until smooth. Stir in 1 tablespoon light corn syrup and refrigerate for about 1 hour. Knead with your fingertips until the chocolate can be rolled out to ⅛ inch thick. Cut with a sharp knife and refrigerate until serving time.

As directed on page 90, prepare the crust, press into a 9-inch pie pan, and bake and cool, or chill to set thoroughly before filling.

Whip the cream until stiff; cover and refrigerate.

Beat the egg whites until soft peaks form. Add the sugar, 1 tablespoon at a time, and beat until stiff but not dry. Reserve.

To make the dark chocolate mousse, combine the chocolate and butter in the top container of a double boiler set over barely simmering water and stir constantly until the chocolate and butter melt. Remove from the heat and whisk in the egg yolks until smooth. Transfer to a bowl and fold in one third of the reserved egg whites, then fold in one third of the whipped cream. Cover and refrigerate for about 2 hours.

Repeat the preceding step to make the milk and the white chocolate mousses, using one half of the remaining egg whites and whipped cream for each mousse. Cover and chill each mousse separately, as above.

Position two tart rings in the pie shell. Fill the smaller ring with the white chocolate mousse and smooth the top with a spatula. Fill the space between the small ring and the larger ring with the milk chocolate mousse and smooth the top. Fill between the ring and the crust with the dark chocolate mousse and smooth the top. Carefully remove the rings and shake the pan to remove any spaces between the mousses. Alternatively, spread the mousses in the pieshell in layers, beginning with the dark and ending with the white. Cover loosely and refrigerate at least 3 hours to firmly set. The pie will keep for up to several days.

Just before serving, garnish the top with the chocolate curls or other chocolate decorations, if using.

**Makes one 9-inch pie; serves 6 to 8.**

# Coffee Crunch Pie

Coffee crunch, used to top a traditional San Francisco cake, adds a wonderful counterpoint to creamy coffee pie filling. This recipe makes more coffee crunch than you'll need for one pie, but the brittle candy keeps well stored in an airtight container for munching or for another pie.

To make the coffee crunch, combine the sugar, coffee, and corn syrup in a deep, heavy saucepan over high heat. Bring to a boil and cook to the hard crack stage or until the mixture measures 310° F on a candy thermometer. Remove from the heat and quickly stir in the baking soda; the mixture will foam furiously. Stir rapidly just until the mixture thickens and pulls away from the side of the pan; do not stir down the foam. Quickly pour onto an ungreased baking sheet or into a shallow 9-inch-square pan; do not spread. Cool until hard, 20 to 30 minutes. Knock the hardened crunch off the sheet or out of the pan, break up into chunks, place between two sheets of waxed paper, and use a rolling pin to crush into coarse crumbs.

As directed on page 90, prepare the crust and line a 9-inch pie pan. Bake and cool, or chill thoroughly to set before filling.

To make the coffee cream filling, combine the egg yolks, sugar, salt, cornstarch, and expresso powder in a heavy saucepan and beat until thick and creamy. Slowly whisk or stir in the milk and cook over medium heat, stirring and scraping the bottom constantly, until the mixture thickens, about 8 to 10 minutes. Reduce the heat to very low and cook until thick, 3 or 4 minutes longer. Remove from the heat, add the butter, and stir until the butter melts. Stir in the liqueur or vanilla. Transfer to a bowl, cover with plastic wrap laid directly on the surface of the custard, and let stand until cool, about 15 minutes.

In a chilled bowl, whip the cream and powdered sugar until fairly stiff but not grainy. Stir about one-third of the whipped cream into the cooled coffee-flavored custard, then fold in the remaining cream and pour into the pieshell. Chill 4 to 6 hours.

Sprinkle with about ½ cup of the coffee crunch just before serving.

**Makes one 9-inch pie; serves 6 to 8.**

COFFEE CRUNCH
1½ cups granulated sugar
¼ cup strong brewed coffee
¼ cup dark corn syrup
3 teaspoons sieved baking soda

Cookie Crumb Crust (page 90)

COFFEE CREAM FILLING
4 egg yolks
¾ cup granulated sugar
¼ teaspoon salt
5 tablespoons cornstarch
2 tablespoons instant espresso
   powder, or to taste
2½ cups milk
2 tablespoons unsalted butter
2 tablespoons coffee-flavored
   liqueur, or 2 teaspoons
   vanilla extract
1 cup heavy (whipping) cream
1 tablespoon powdered sugar

# Canadian Maple Sugar Pie

½ recipe Basic Pie Crust (page 10)
¼ cup all-purpose flour, preferably
   unbleached
1 cup granulated maple sugar, or
   ¾ cup packed brown sugar mixed
   with ¼ cup maple syrup
¼ teaspoon salt
1½ cups heavy (whipping) cream,
   light cream, or half-and-half
3 tablespoons unsalted butter,
   cut into small pieces
Additional maple sugar for sprinkling
   (optional)

Toronto-based food writer Anita Stewart suggested the use of maple sugar, whenever possible, for this simple old favorite, which is especially delicious for a special breakfast or afternoon tea. Since granulated maple sugar is often difficult to locate, light brown sugar blended with a bit of maple syrup makes a good substitute. Granulated white sugar may also be used.

As directed beginning on page 10, prepare the pastry, roll it out, line a 9-inch pie pan, and partially bake. Cool the pie shell about 15 minutes before filling.

Preheat an oven to 350° F.

Mix the flour with the sugar and salt and spread the mixture evenly over the bottom of the cooled baked pie shell. Pour the cream over the top and draw a spoon through several times to mix. Dot the top with the butter. Cover the rim of the pastry with aluminum foil strips to prevent overbrowning.

Bake until the filling is set to the touch and beginning to turn golden brown, about 45 minutes. Transfer to a wire rack to cool for about 15 minutes. Sprinkle with additional sugar, if desired. Serve at room temperature.

**Makes one 9-inch double-crust pie; serves 6 to 8.**

# Caramel Pie

½ recipe Basic Pie Crust (page 10), or
    1 recipe Coconut Crust (page 91)
4 egg yolks (reserve whites
    for topping)
1½ cups granulated sugar
¼ teaspoon salt
6 tablespoons cornstarch
2 cups milk
⅓ cup water
½ cup (1 stick) unsalted butter
1½ teaspoons vanilla extract
Meringue Topping (page 92)

**This has been a McNair family favorite for decades.**

As directed beginning on page 10 or page 91, prepare the pastry, roll it out, line a 9-inch pie pan, and bake completely. Cool the pie shell about 15 minutes before filling.

In a heavy saucepan, combine the egg yolks, ½ cup of the sugar, salt, and cornstarch and mix thoroughly. Slowly whisk or stir in the milk and cook over medium heat, stirring constantly, until thickened, about 8 to 10 minutes. Reduce the heat to very low and cook until quite thick, 3 or 4 minutes longer.

Meanwhile, combine the remaining 1 cup sugar and the water in a small stainless-steel, uncoated copper, or heavy aluminum saucepan (avoid tinned copper or enameled pans). Place over medium heat and cook until the sugar is melted and the mixture is the color of mahogany, about 10 to 15 minutes; shake the pan occasionally to distribute heat, but do not stir the mixture.

Remove the custard mixture from the heat and drizzle in the caramelized sugar, stirring or whisking constantly. Add the butter and stir until the butter melts. Stir in the vanilla. Transfer to a bowl, cover with plastic wrap laid directly on the surface of the custard, and let stand until cool, about 15 minutes.

Preheat an oven to 350° F.

Spoon the custard into the cooled shell. Top with meringue and bake until lightly browned, 10 to 15 minutes. Remove to a wire rack and cool. Serve warm or at room temperature.

**Makes one 9-inch pie; serves 6 to 8.**

VARIATION: For a butterscotch pie, prepare the custard with 1 cup packed brown sugar. Eliminate the melted sugar.

# Fried Dried Fruit Pies

A special memory from my childhood is of these old-time turnover pies that my Grandmother Olivia Belle Keith made from apples dried on backyard screens during hot Mississippi summers. Mamaw always made the pliable crust with lard and fried the pies in lard. While it's hard to beat that flavor, those with cholesterol problems should use solid all-vegetable shortening in the pastry and either fry them in polyunsaturated oil or brush the pastry with beaten egg white and bake them in a preheated 400° F oven until golden, about 15 to 20 minutes.

To make the filling, place the fruit in a large saucepan and add enough cold water to almost cover. Bring to a boil over medium-high heat. Reduce the heat to low, cover, and simmer until quite tender. Mash the fruit or coarsely purée in a food processor. Return the fruit to a saucepan and sweeten to taste; the amount of sugar will vary depending on the fruit. Add compatible spices to taste. Cook, uncovered, over medium-low heat until the mixture is quite thick. Cool to room temperature.

To make the pastry, sift the flour and baking powder together into a mixing bowl. Add the melted lard or shortening, eggs, and just enough milk to make a stiff dough. Turn out onto a lightly floured work surface and knead, adding flour a little at a time if necessary, until no longer sticky, about 5 minutes. With a heavy rolling pin, roll dough out to about ⅛ inch thick. Using a 5½-inch saucer as a guide, cut out about 10 circles with a sharp knife. Roll out each circle as thinly as possible with a few more strokes.

Spoon about 3 tablespoons of the cooled filling onto one half of each dough round, moisten the edges of the dough with cold water, fold the other half over the filling, and press the edges together. Crimp the edges with the tines of a fork or a fluted pastry sealer.

Melt the lard or pour the oil to a depth of about 2 inches in a deep-fat fryer or deep, heavy skillet and heat to 375° F, or until a cube of bread turns golden brown in about 1 minute. Fry a few pies at a time, turning occasionally, until golden brown all around, about 5 minutes. Remove to paper toweling to drain and cool. Sprinkle with sugar if desired and serve warm or at room temperature.

**Makes about 10 pies; serves 6 to 10.**

FRUIT FILLING
12 ounces dried apples, apricots, stemmed figs, peaches, pears, or pitted prunes
Granulated sugar to taste
Ground cinnamon, cloves, or ginger, or freshly grated nutmeg to taste

PASTRY
4 cups all-purpose flour, preferably unbleached
2 teaspoons baking powder
½ cup lard or solid vegetable shortening, melted and cooled
2 eggs, lightly beaten
About ¾ cup milk

Lard or high-quality vegetable oil for deep-frying
Powdered or granulated sugar for dusting (optional)

# Peanut Satin Pie

Cookie Crumb Crust (page 90),
  preferably made with gingersnaps
8 ounces cream cheese, at room
  temperature
¾ cup smooth peanut butter, at
  room temperature
6 tablespoons unsalted butter, at
  room temperature
2 egg yolks
1 can (14 ounces) sweetened
  condensed milk
1 teaspoon vanilla extract
Chopped unsalted roasted peanuts
  for garnish

**The name comes from the ultra-smooth texture; use an electric mixer to achieve this consistency. Serve with warm Bittersweet Chocolate Sauce (page 93).**

Prepare the crust as directed on page 90 and bake and cool, or refrigerate to set completely.

Combine the cream cheese, peanut butter, butter, and egg yolks in a large bowl and beat until fluffy. While beating, drizzle in the condensed milk and beat until smooth. Stir in the vanilla. Pour into the pie shell, cover loosely, and refrigerate until the filling is firm and well chilled, about 2 hours.

Sprinkle with peanuts before serving.

**Makes one 9-inch pie; serves 6 to 8.**

# SPECIAL CRUSTS

## Cookie Crumb Crust

A food processor or blender makes fast work of turning cookies into crumbs. As a general rule, 8 ounces of whole cookies equals 2 cups of crumbs. Adjust the amount of sugar and spice to suit the cookie type. Crushed cereals such as oat bran flakes can be used instead of cookie crumbs. Substitute finely ground nuts for a portion of the crumbs, if desired.

2 cups fine cookie crumbs, from graham crackers, vanilla wafers, gingersnaps, amaretti, chocolate wafers, dry macaroons, or other crisp cookies
¼ cup granulated, powdered, or packed brown sugar
6 tablespoons (¾ stick) unsalted butter, melted
½ teaspoon ground cinnamon, ginger, or nutmeg (optional)

Preheat an oven to 350° F.

Combine the crumbs, sugar, butter, and spice, if using, in a large bowl and stir to blend thoroughly. Spread in a well-buttered 9-inch pie pan and press with your fingertips to pack the mixture evenly on the bottom and sides of the pan. Or press an 8-inch pie pan into the mixture and press down to distribute and compact the crust. Use your fingertips to press the rim to form smooth edges.

To set the crust, bake for 10 minutes; cool to room temperature before filling. Or set by covering the unbaked crust with plastic wrap and refrigerating for 30 minutes before filling.

**Makes one 9-inch pie crust.**

## Coconut Crust

Either fresh or dried coconut works well in this flavorful crust.

4 cups shredded coconut
6 tablespoons (¾ stick) unsalted
    butter, softened

Preheat an oven to 325° F.

Combine the coconut and softened butter in a large bowl and stir or mix with your fingertips to thoroughly combine. Spread in a well-buttered 9-inch pie pan and press with your fingertips to pack the mixture evenly on the bottom and sides of the pan.

Bake until golden brown, about 15 minutes. Add aluminum foil strips around the rim if it begins to get too brown. Transfer to a wire rack and chill completely before filling.

**Makes one 9-inch pie crust.**

## Nut Crust

Almonds, hazelnuts, macadamias, pecans, and walnuts make wonderful crunchy crusts that are good with light, creamy fillings.

¾ cup (about 6 ounces) finely
    ground nuts
1¼ cup all-purpose flour,
    preferably unbleached
3 tablespoons granulated sugar
½ cup (1 stick) unsalted butter,
    melted
1 teaspoon almond extract
1 egg white, lightly beaten

In a large bowl, combine the nuts, flour, and sugar. Stir in the melted butter, almond extract, and beaten egg white and mix thoroughly. Spread in a well-buttered 9-inch pie pan and press with your fingertips to pack the mixture evenly on the bottom and sides of the pan. Or press an 8-inch pie pan into the mixture and press down to distribute and compact the crust. Using your fingertips, press the rim to form smooth edges. Refrigerate for about 30 minutes.

Preheat an oven to 350° F.

Bake until golden brown, 20 to 25 minutes; cover the rim with strips of foil if the crust begins to get too brown. Remove to a wire rack to cool completely before filling.

**Makes one 9-inch crust.**

## Meringue Crust

A change-of-pace crust to fill with cooled custard, mousse, or lightly sweetened fresh berries topped with whipped cream.

4 egg whites
½ teaspoon cream of tartar
1 cup granulated sugar, preferably
    superfine

Preheat an oven to 275° F.

In a large bowl, beat the egg whites until frothy. Beat in the cream of tartar. Beat in the sugar, about 1 tablespoon at a time, until the whites are stiff but not dry.

Transfer to a buttered 9-inch pie pan, spreading so the meringue is about ¼ to ½ inch thick on the bottom and about 1 inch thick on the sides. Bake until firm to the touch and lightly browned, about 1 hour. Transfer to a wire rack and cool completely before filling. The crust will shrink and may crack during the cooling.

**Makes one 9-inch pie crust.**

# TOPPINGS

## *Meringue Topping*

Double or triple the recipe for cloudlike "mile-high" presentations.

Since the topping contains cream of tartar to stabilize the meringue, do not beat the egg whites in a copper-lined bowl; the chemical reaction will turn the egg white greenish. Aluminum bowls will turn the mixture gray.

5 egg whites (about ⅔ cup)
½ teaspoon cream of tartar
Pinch of salt
½ cup granulated sugar, preferably superfine
1 teaspoon vanilla extract

Preheat an oven to 350° F.

Place the egg whites in a stainless steel bowl set over simmering water and heat until warm to the touch. Beat until foamy. Add the cream of tartar and salt and continue beating until the whites form soft peaks. Add the sugar, 1 tablespoon at a time, beating well after each addition. Beat in the vanilla and continue beating until stiff, glossy peaks form. Spread the meringue over the filling, making sure the meringue touches the inner edge of the pastry to prevent weeping and shrinkage. Using a spatula or knife blade, swirl the top of the egg whites decoratively. Bake until lightly browned, about 10 minutes.

To prevent shrinkage of the baked meringue, transfer the pie to a draft-free place that is not too cold and let stand until serving. Do not refrigerate.

**Makes enough for one 9-inch pie.**

## *Whipped Cream*

When you plan to serve cream as an accompaniment to slices of pie, whip it until it just holds its shape; this is known as Crème Chantilly. For folding into a pie filling or covering the top of a chilled pie, whip the cream stiffer, but avoid overbeating, which causes graininess. The cornstarch in powdered, or confectioner's, sugar helps stabilize the cream when you add liqueur or other liquid flavorings.

1 cup very cold heavy (whipping) cream, not ultra-pasteurized
About 2 tablespoons (or to taste) granulated sugar, preferably superfine, or powdered sugar
½ teaspoon vanilla extract, or 2 teaspoons liqueur or spirits, or cooled melted chocolate, or pureed fruits or fruit syrup to taste

Pour the cream into a chilled bowl and beat with a wire whisk or electric hand mixer until it just begins to thicken. Add sugar and vanilla or other flavoring and continue whipping to the desired stage; be very careful not to overbeat when using an electric mixer.

**Makes about 2 cups.**

## Custard Sauce
## (Crème Anglaise)

There's no better accompaniment to warm fruit or chocolate fudge pie than this creamy custard sauce. For a richer flavor, substitute heavy cream for half of the milk. Strips of orange or lemon zest can be used in place of the vanilla, if a delicate citrus flavor is desired.

2 cups milk
½ vanilla bean, split, or 1 to
    2 teaspoons vanilla extract
4 egg yolks, at room temperature
½ cup granulated sugar

Combine the milk and vanilla bean, if using, in a heavy saucepan over medium heat and bring almost to a boil; if using vanilla extract, reserve for later use.

In the top container of a double boiler, whisk or beat the egg yolks and sugar to blend well. While whisking, gradually add the heated milk; transfer the vanilla bean to the mixture. Place over simmering water and whisk until the custard registers 170 to 175° F on a candy thermometer or thickens to the density of a creamy sauce, about 15 minutes. It should coat the back of a spoon, and your finger should leave a trail when you run it across the spoon.

Strain the mixture through a fine wire sieve into a bowl. Add the vanilla bean or stir in the vanilla extract to taste, if using. Place a piece of plastic wrap or waxed paper directly on the surface of the custard. Cool to room temperature, then refrigerate until well chilled, as long as overnight. Remove the vanilla bean before serving.

Makes about 2 cups.

## Warm Cinnamon
## Cider Sauce

Serve over apple or pear pie.

2 tablespoons unsalted butter
1 tablespoon all-purpose flour,
    preferably unbleached
2 cups apple cider
2 teaspoons ground cinnamon

Melt the butter in a saucepan over low heat. Whisk in the flour and cook, stirring constantly, for about 3 minutes. Slowly whisk in the cider and stir until smooth. Add the cinnamon and cook, stirring constantly, for about 2 minutes. Serve warm.

Makes about 2 cups.

## Bittersweet Chocolate
## Sauce

Use the finest chocolate available. Part or all semisweet chocolate produces a sweeter sauce.

8 ounces bittersweet chocolate,
    chopped
2 tablespoons unsalted butter
1 cup heavy (whipping) cream
1 teaspoon vanilla extract

Combine the chocolate, butter, and cream in a heavy saucepan over low heat and cook, stirring frequently, until the chocolate is melted and the mixture is smooth. Stir in the vanilla extract and cool to room temperature, or refrigerate, then reheat just to warm before serving.

Makes about 1½ cups.

# INDEX

# RECIPE INDEX

# ACKNOWLEDGMENTS

To Jack Jensen and his staff at Chronicle Books. It seems fitting that a baking book round out our first dozen books together.

To those who shared favorite pie recipes, ideas, or props: Matilda Adams, Eula Cain, Ruth Dosher, Brooksley Kersey, Marian May, Lucille McNair, Marilyn Retzer, Kristi Spence, Anita Stewart, and James Wentworth.

To Robert Lambert, author of *Fantasy Chocolate Desserts,* for the chocolate decoration technique on page 78.

To Carolyn Miller for her copy editing of my words.

To Ellen Quan for her excellent help in the studio kitchen.

To Patricia Brabant and her assistant M. J. Murphy for painting the rich backgrounds as well as once again making magic with the camera.

To my San Francisco and Lake Tahoe friends and family who remain supportive through this and every time-consuming project, especially to D. Arvid Adams, John Carr, Glen Carroll, Jan Ellis, Louis Hicks, the Ken High family, Louis Hicks, Al Horton, Meri McEneny, Martha and Devereux McNair, Stephen Marcus, Marian and Alan May, Jack Porter, Douglas Jackson, Mark Leno, Jeffrey Fraenkel, John Richardson, the Bob Spence family, and Stephen Suzman.

To Addie Prey, Buster Booroo, Joshua J. Chew, Michael T. Wigglebutt, and Dweasel Pickle at The Rockpile Press who make every day as sweet as pie.

To Lin Cotton for making my life and my work seem as easy as pie.